Grief
Relief

Healing Activities For Coping With Loss

VALENCIA MCMAHON

WESTBOW
PRESS®
A DIVISION OF THOMAS NELSON
& ZONDERVAN

WestBow Press books may be ordered through booksellers or by contacting:

WestBow Press
A Division of Thomas Nelson & Zondervan
1663 Liberty Drive
Bloomington, IN 47403
www.westbowpress.com
844-714-3454

ISBN: 978-1-6642-5208-0 (sc)
ISBN: 978-1-6642-5207-3 (e)

Print information available on the last page.

WestBow Press rev. date: 01/14/2022

Contents

Dedication vii
Introduction.. ix

SECTION I

Outdoors Activities 1
Indoor Activities.. 12

SECTION II

Allow Yourself Plenty of Time to Grieve 27
These are the No's No's 32
The Light Will Shine Again.. 38
Learn to Enjoy Life Again 41
Additional Activities.. 43

Writing Exercises.. 45
About the Author 47

Dedication

This book is dedicated to my mother who taught me about the love of God since I was a child. To my sisters who thought the world of me, and to my loving husband who was always there for me with his beautiful smile and quiet strength. I Thank God for Their Love

This book is also dedicated to my Lord and Savior Jesus Christ. Though much was taken from me, I know that so much more was given to me by the one who loves me the most.

Thank you, Jesus, for your everlasting love.

Introduction

Suffering a loss great or small can often leave you facing an uphill battle that may not be easy to climb. The climb is especially hard when the loss is someone to which you had a significant bond with, or great affection for. But even in our deepest pain, we should not despair. Grief is our body's natural response to loss. You will undoubtedly experience an array of emotions during that process and no two people are alike. Though we spend little time thinking about them, there are spiritual, physical, and behavioral aspects as well to grief that we must not forget. For there to be true healing, we must treat the whole person by treating the mind, body and soul.

In all cases though, it is good to know that we have hope. There are lots of professional organizations, programs and perhaps even books that are designed to help those who may need professional assistance. This guide however; is not intended to give professional advice and should not be taken as such. It is only a compilation of some of the things that I have found, that when I put them into practice, proved to be a tremendous help to me. While all of these suggestions may not be for everyone, you may find that some of them are exactly what you need. I strongly encourage you to try them and see for yourself. Who knows, you may be surprised. But before we talk about the healing exercises, we'll take a glimpse at what I've noticed over the years on how I grieved during my losses. The experiences were as unique as my relationship with those I lost. I learned something we all should remember: to be kind to ourselves. Don't impose any time limits on your healing process. Let it take as long as it takes. Know that there is no 'normal' or prescribed amount of time to grieve. From my own experience of watching myself and my family members, I can tell you that the grieving process was different depending on the age group, what we believed, and even the way we thought. It was in that time that I came to realize that the people in my support network often knowingly and unknowingly played a role in my healing process.

Embrace the pain when it is from the loss of a loved one. They are worthy of your grief, so don't hold back; however, do not despair. You will experience happiness and hope again. You will find that while there is no getting back to the normal you once knew, you can move forward and resume some of your regular routines. Life is for the living, so by the grace of God, live it.

When I lost my husband, the grief that I experienced at that time and the grief I still experience from time to time are vastly different from the grief I felt when I lost my mother, both of my sisters, and two of my brothers. I'm sure this would ring true for most, if not everyone, who suffered a loss. Let's see if you can recognize any of these feelings.

Spouse – If your loss is your spouse, then you will understand how this particular loss can be the hardest, even though it is possible to remarry at a later date. When I first met my husband, I knew he would be the man I would marry. The connection and kindred spirit were instant. It was as if God had sent him especially for me. When we finally got married, the thought was that we'd be together for many years to come. But there is this thing called life that constantly gets in the way. I never thought that I would lose him six months after marriage. I found myself having to face that otherwise bright future alone without the man who had planned to be by my side. That future that once looked so bright now had hues of grey. I had to figure out how to make it without the person who had for ten and a half years stood by my side as my best friend and confidant. He was that solid shoulder I always cried on. He was that voice of reason and optimism when I needed it. Facing the weeks, months, and years ahead without your spouse will no doubt require all the courage you can summon, especially around birthdays and holidays, nevertheless have courage and allow life to happen again.

Siblings – What about when you lose a sibling. Are those emotions the same as losing a spouse? After the loss of both sisters, a few days apart, my mood swing went from having faith in God to questioning if He even existed. In my experience, the emotions are vastly different. Note that the feelings, although they may be different, are no less painful, no less honest, or no less critical. I was utterly speechless when I lost both of my sisters back to back. I'm still wondering how this sort of thing happens in the world. Many nights I wondered if I would be next. You know the wild things our minds can dream up when we're hurting or have fear. Unlike a spouse, you can't get another sister or brother when both parents are deceased. If you were incredibly close to them, words could not express how hard it is without them. If we are not careful, we can easily overlook the emotions of a grieving sibling.

Parent – When it comes to losing our parents, where we are in our adulthood when the loss occurs can determine how we deal with the loss. God had blessed my mother with long life, and I would have loved to see her have more years. When I lost my mother, the pain was not less just because she lived a long life; however, it made the loss easier to accept because she had had a long life. Thankfully, all of us were mature adults, and so for us, her death was the natural progression of life, notwithstanding the disease that took her life. But, I've seen with my nieces and nephews that children who lose their parents at a young age may experience that loss differently since they did not get the advantage to cultivate a long and loving relationship with their parents. So while the mature adults grieved for wanting more of what we had, the younger adults and children grieved for what they never had. Navigating this type of loss, especially at an early age, could require the assistance of a professional.

We should never fear seeking professional assistance in any of these types of losses. Keep in mind there are many sources for help to guide us through our grief. We need to open ourselves up and ask for it.

A Time for Everything

³ There is a time for everything,
and a season for every activity under the heavens:
² a time to be born and a time to die,
a time to plant and a time to uproot,
³ a time to kill and a time to heal,
a time to tear down and a time to build,
⁴ a time to weep and a time to laugh,
a time to mourn and a time to dance,
⁵ a time to scatter stones and a time to gather them,
a time to embrace and a time to refrain from embracing,
⁶ a time to search and a time to give up,
a time to keep and a time to throw away,
⁷ a time to tear and a time to mend,
a time to be silent and a time to speak,
⁸ a time to love and a time to hate,
a time for war and a time for peace.

Ecclesiastes 3:1-8

Section I

Outdoors Activities

Besides taking routine walks through my neighborhood and on the beach with my husband, I was not necessarily an outdoor person. After losing multiple family members, though, I found that I would often get out of the house to get a different perspective on things. My husband taught me that. No matter how disquieted my spirit felt on the inside, I knew I needed to continue moving forward while still holding memories in my heart. I can't tell you how many times I've heard that taking care of yourself is, first and foremost, the most important thing to do when you're grieving. It sounds like a no-brainer, right. Well, let me tell you that it's not as easy as it sounds.

During some of my grieving, I often forgot to eat correctly, or I would sometimes forget to eat at all. When I did, it was very little food. I realized that all of the things that I'd used to do with my loved ones that brought me contentment, I no longer cared to do. So, with full knowledge that I needed to feed the well, I decided to take action. I focused on remembering the things I used to do with or without them that once brought me joy. I particularly enjoy going to the beach and listening to the sound of the waves or just sitting on the lanai, listening to the sound of the water fountain.

The more I thought of my late husband, the more I remembered how encouraging he was, even when things got tough. I decided to act. Over the following pages, I will share what I did that helped me through my grief. They include activities for the Body, Mind, and Spirit. So come on and put on those tennis shoes, buy that ticket, or plant that tree. The choice is yours. Whatever you do, go ahead and get out there. If you need to, take a friend. Remember 'you got this. Here are some outdoor activities I've enjoyed doing. You may want to give them a try as well. Remember, there are scores of outdoor activities you can do to uplift your spirit, so if it's not one of these, check out the other suggestion at the back of this guide.

A time to weep and a time to laugh
Ecclesiastes 3:4

Take a walk in your neighborhood. Nature has a very natural and therapeutic way to help us heal. Before my husband passed away, we enjoyed taking an early morning or leisurely evening walks through the neighborhood. Something about being outside in the fresh air makes your senses come alive. The crisp morning air or those warm breezy nights made me more aware of my surroundings. The neighborhood where I lived had an inviting terrain, making me want to go outside and enjoy it. Often I would stand on the deck and survey the woods in the backyard or take a leisurely glance at the mountains in the distance.

The walks may have been therapeutic, but there were other benefits. Walking always gave me energy. It's supposed to strengthen your heart and even help extend your life, and that's to name a few. This one is free, so why not give it a try.

Take a walk in the woods. You can listen to the sound of the leaves rustling in the wind or the crisp crackle underneath your feet. Although there were woods in the back of the house I lived in, I preferred walking in the woods at the nearby parks. You can find a great deal of beauty walking in the woods. The natural elements always had a subtle pull that just worked for me. Aside from the apparent beauty of the woods, the sound of silence with a bit of nature mixed in made it even more beautiful. The unmistakable smell of the pine trees assaulted my senses and stimulated my brain. Nature, with its unfiltered beauty, never failed to uplift my spirit. That's why I always loved it there. Try and see if it does the same for your spirit. Isn't it about time you took that walk? Some of the benefits of this activity are that it can boost the immune system, lower blood pressure, increase the ability to focus, boost mood, and improve sleep.

Watch a sunrise, then bask in its warmth. There is a lot to be said about the healing properties of the sun. It's also an excellent source of vitamin D. This was hand down the most favorite thing my husband and I enjoyed doing together. After he passed, it was hard for me at first, but once I allowed myself to cherish the memories, it became the balm that helped heal my soul. The pain was still there, but the beauty and peace were undeniable. God made the sun for a perfect reason, so get out there and enjoy it. Some of the benefits of basking in the sun are that it can reduce stress, help maintain strong bones, helps with sleep, strengthens the immune system, and helps with the production of vitamin D.

Refresh your sense of smell with a bit of scent therapy by inhaling the marvelous aroma of freshly cut grass. It may sound a little strange but try it. That rich aroma that we smell is actually from a chemical compound that is released called green leaf volatiles (GLS's). The grass healing itself from the injury inflicted by the lawnmower causes this natural reaction. There's something special about nature, especially when you can smell it. I believe it helps ground you to mother earth. Remember, God did make us from the dust of the ground. The benefit I found is that it can help trigger memories. For example, every time I smelled one of my husband's shirts, I thought of fond memories of both of us together.

Have a walk in the rain. Have you ever sat inside your house and watched the rain pouring down and you allowed your mind to wander? I can't tell you the countless times I've done that. My husband and I would find a prime spot for viewing. Sometimes we would stand on the lanai and let the gentle rain fall on our faces. It smelt like heaven. These days if I'm outside and the rain isn't heavy, you can bet I will enjoy it. I'm one of those people who would walk to my car in the gentle rain shower rather than run for cover. If you feel inclined to do your walk in rain gear, go right ahead and feed that inclination. The best benefit for me about walking in the rain without the one I love is it reduces stress. I also found that it's a great time to cry cause no one will be able to tell if you're crying. Some other benefits of the rain are it's calming, soothing, and can help you relax. I understand it's good for hair and skin and can change your perspective. Considering the rain can do all of that, who wouldn't want to get wet outside.

Surround yourself with living things. One of the things that I started doing after losing my husband was surrounding myself with many living plants. I wasn't the best at keeping them alive for extended periods (my husband was good at that), but because I loved the sweet aroma of plants like lavender, lilies, and gardenia, I kept them around. In addition to stimulating the senses, they also provide better air quality since plants can remove certain toxins from the air. They can help promote a sense of wellbeing, and they can also promote healing and productivity. Who knew? For the designer in you, they also add color to any room. Don't have a green thumb, why not take a trip to your local nursery and inhale their sweet aroma.

Be adventurous. Take a group trip or go out by yourself to a place you've wanted to go but never took the time. After losing my loved ones, I stayed put and did not go anywhere I didn't have to go. For a while, I allowed my fears to cripple me. But once I tried getting out there and taking on the adventure, I realized it invigorated me. I felt alive again. You don't need to travel to another country to experience an adventure. There are plenty of adventures to be found in your backyard. Find yourself a nearby historic town, check it out, or take that hike up a mountain or slide down a waterfall. Whatever adventure you decide to take on, do it with your whole heart. Being adventurous helped me become more confident. It mentally helped prepare me for change and the subsequent challenges in my life.

Plant a tree. What better way to have the memory of your loved ones live on than this? Perhaps as a teenager, you carved your initials on a tree or bench and swore that your love would last forever. Planting a tree is an excellent way to share that love with others. There are numerous benefits to planting trees. Trees can provide food, shelter, and a home for humans and wildlife alike. Finally, trees help keep cities cool, and they prevent water pollution. Planting a tree is a beautiful way to keep love alive. I am looking forward to planting my next tree.

Indoor Activities

If like me, you find that you are not necessarily the outdoor type, that's quite all right. I found myself searching for activities that I could do indoors. I am not a fan of being outside when it's sweltering, which fueled my need to find indoor activities that were equally engaging and delivered just as much satisfaction. On the following pages, I have listed some indoor activities that you can try that can get your inner spirit in harmony: Like me, I hope you will find comfort in exercising any number of them.

Go on and Get Spiritual. Yes, I said get spiritual. You've already gotten physical with your activities; now it's time to give your inner spirit some love. You may frown at this idea, especially if you have feelings of anger. After I lost my last sister, getting spiritual was the last thing on my mind because I blamed God for the loss. After months of pain and turmoil, I regained my ability to reason and realized that my grieving was absolutely the best time to bring God in. There have been studies that show that strengthening your spiritual life can help a person cope with grief and get through grief better. It worked for me. If I did not come to feel God's comfort through His Holy Spirit, my state of mind during my grieving process would not be as it is today. Times were tough, but I made the most of the hours I spent indoors. For me, the best benefit was building a trusting, lasting, and confident relationship with God. By finding peace within, I was able to live in harmony with others.

Search for A Deeper Meaning. With why being the most unanswered question when grieving, I decided to go beyond that. I told myself to search for meaning. To get anywhere near a sense of being content, I started asking myself questions that would guide me down paths I had not previously taken. I asked myself questions that would help me determine my purpose. I wanted to know, after so much loss, what things mattered most to me. So I asked, and then I listened. Jesus tells us that we will find Him when we search for Him with all of our hearts. So I did.

Losing my two sisters and then my mother was very hard. I was grateful to have my fiancé, soon-to-be husband, by my side to help me cope. He was my biggest supporter. I always felt like God had placed him with me to support my endeavors, encourage me in my dreams, and show me a different way to see things. Most of all, he was that all-important shoulder to lean on in difficult times. Losing him was the proverbial straw that broke the camel's back. When I lost him, I lost me. I couldn't understand how God could put him in my life, then allow him to be gone so quickly. I wasn't angry with God; I just needed some answers. I needed something to make sense. How does one go from being completely happy to a sense of utter loss? I was a ship adrift at sea, going whichever way the wind carried me. As the winds began to die down, I knew I had to decide what direction I wanted to continue. I sought the only one I knew that could help me. With no husband to communicate with, I turned to God and I talked to him. I shared my fears, my sorrows, and my dreams. I told Him everything I needed and wanted. Most of all, I told Him I needed and wanted Him in my life. The more I talked to Him, the more confident I felt that He was attentive to my words.

The death of my loved ones changed me. It changed my attitude along with my outlook on life. But, most importantly, it changed me spiritually. When I look back over that period, I can see a loving God who loved me so much more than I understood at the time. That also changed me. It didn't take away the pain from my losses, but it changed me. My ups and downs, challenges and difficulties, gains and losses all paled in light of the cross. I saw that I could complain about many things, but why, when salvation and eternity were mine for the taking.

It's been three and a half years since I lost my husband, and I still have my talks with God. And you know what, He answers me. I have assurance in His word that all will get restored to the glory He originally intended for it to be. What a glorious reunion it will be. Not only will I see my loved ones' faces again, but I will be able to live throughout eternity with them.

What are you going to search for a better understanding of?

_____

_____

_____

_____

_____

_____

_____

_____

_____

_____

_____

_____

One way to help us cope with the loss of a loved one is to **write fond letters** to honor them. I'm sure in your life you've felt sad because you held something in, but as soon as you let it out, you felt better. This exercise should have the same effect. I wrote a sweet letter to my late husband. It wasn't easy, though, knowing that he would never read it. The benefit for me is that it makes me smile every time I read it. Some have been told to do this exercise and then burn the letter. But how do you burn something so full of love? I didn't burn my letter. If you can hold on to it without holding on to the past, keep it tucked away for that rainy day when you need a pick me up. While it may bring intense emotions that are hard to handle at first, if you stick with it, you may find that it can have therapeutic benefits by allowing you to share, say, and express your grief through conversation.

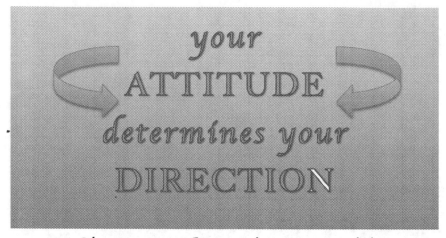

Change it, and you change your life

Change your attitude. Those who've discovered that our attitude changes the way we see things realize that if we want to see positively, we have to think that way. I genuinely believe that when we change our attitude to be positive, our whole life changes. That is why I say, 'change it, and you change your life.' Things got rough for me after my loved ones died. I was sure that nothing good was on the radar for me. I remembered my husband was always thinking positively. I adopted that line of thought and started focusing on positive things. That made things so much easier for me. It became my way of life. That is not to say that negative things don't exist still, but by focusing on staying positive, your outlook on life is different in a positive way, of course. No negative Nellie's here. The benefits are a longer life span, a lower rate of depression, and distress. Better psychological and physical well-being.

What attitude(s) do you want to change?

_____

_____

_____

_____

_____

_____

_____

_____

_____

_____

_____

_____

_____

_____

Take up Yoga. Growing up, I was very athletic. I loved running track, and I played on both the softball and volleyball team at my school. In my adult years, I found activities that took a little less stress on the body. I found that Yoga is beneficial in reducing the physical and emotional strain on the mind and body. It uses your physical and mental focus to create peace of body and mind. So if you prefer to get bent into shape rather than bent out of shape, then Yoga might do the trick. But don't get it twisted. Namaste.

Meditation. Now that you have a prayerful attitude, start spending some extended time in a quiet place where you can relax and clear your mind. You want to clear your mind so you can focus on God. For example, after losing my loved ones, I spent a lot of quiet time alone. During this time, I started reading and meditating on God's word. It brought comfort to me that nothing else had up until that time. To help me meditate, I used techniques like breathing, music, and candlelight. In addition, you can add some of my favorite scents to excite the senses, such as lavender, vanilla, and lemongrass. These can be great tools to assist you in your meditation.

Pray, Pray, Pray. Prayer for help, in my opinion, is the most important of these exercises. In the end, it's all we have. You can't get spiritual without prayer. There is no time like the present to find out what you believe. The bible says we have not because we ask not. So ask God for acceptance and peace. Prayer was the glue that kept my life together during those times. It still keeps me grounded today. I've learned to always be in a prayerful mindset. You don't need to always be on your knees to pray. God is ready to listen to us anytime we want to talk to Him. Isaiah 65:24, says 'That before they call, I will answer; and while they are still speaking, I will hear.' The benefits that I enjoyed from adding prayer to my daily life is that it changed my focus from my pain to the one that can take away my pain. Prayer helps us build a relationship with God by bringing us closer to him. It ushers us into God's presence. It's also a way to help others when we pray with someone and pray for someone. The most important thing that prayer did for me was bring about change. Just as I have enjoyed these benefits, I know you will enjoy these and many more.

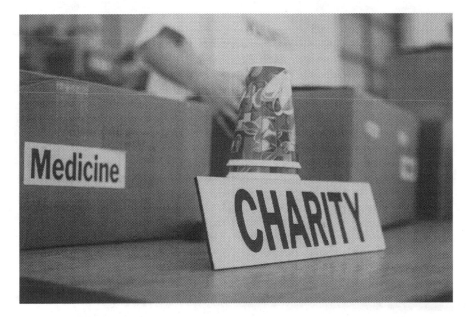

Take time to help others. I can't stress enough how much getting involved with helping others has helped me heal. It's amazing how you discover that when you spend time helping others, you forget how much pain you're feeling. I think God made us that way. Reaching out to help others will help you reach beyond yourself. You're sure to find greater meaning in life. I discovered things that I had not previously known. As I pursued my spiritual life, I've found that there was an awakening and a renewed sense of brotherly love. My husband often donated to charities, so I started a foundation in his name on his birthday to continue that. One of the most significant emotional satisfaction is when I reach out to others grieving. Like me, I hope that when you find you can reach out to others and smile, you realize that you have started on your journey forward. Jesus said in Matthew 25:40, 'Inasmuch as ye have done it unto one of the least of these my brethren; ye have done it unto me.' I read that helping others can foster a sense of belonging, boost your self-esteem and help you live longer. These are excellent reasons for helping other people.

What can you do to help other?

_____

_____

_____

_____

_____

_____

_____

_____

_____

_____

_____

_____

_____

Section II

Allow Yourself Plenty
of Time to Grieve

The period after a loss can be difficult for people who are not grieving to understand. Often, we are only given a few days off in our work life, which does very little for those suffering. When you consider that grief can last anywhere between 18 months to 5 years or longer, you must wonder how people are coping with the loss. I can tell you it was not easy for me. It was difficult for me to focus on things, whether at work or somewhere else. I always felt like I was somewhere else. For the sake of my sanity, I had to take each day as it came. There are days when I feel like I can make it, then wham, reality reminds me that someone is missing in my life. I'm back in the dumps again to start over when that happens. But I do start over with continuing my journey forward.

Don't feel like you have to hurry up and get back to normal because there is no getting back to normal. After my mother died, I was financially sound, so I left my job. I needed time to figure out where do I go next. If you can swing it financially, take an extended leave. Whatever you do, leave the guilt behind. Again, give yourself plenty of time to heal at your own pace. Over the following pages are some activities you can try. I can't tell you how much these have helped me.

Take time out. For those who experience grief by losing a loved one, keeping busy can seem like an excellent solution to not thinking about the loss. While this can be true, it may not be the best course of action. After my husband died, I didn't know what to do. My two sisters were gone, my mother was gone, and now he was gone. That realization was too much for my brain to handle. I decided I'd keep busy to avoid thinking about this unwanted new reality that had broken down my walls of happiness.

After weeks of keeping busier than any bee, I had a breakthrough. I discovered that keeping busy only fueled my denial and prolonged my healing. You need to slow down and take some time out for yourself. No rule says you have to pretend that everything is ok when you lose someone. Especially when that someone was close to you. I found that when I took time to reflect, I could begin to heal. Now, when I think of them, I feel blessed with the flood of memories of my time with them.

Shed Tears of Love. Priceless is the cost of a good cry, not to mention its necessity. Crying is essential in our grieving process. It relieves the body of chemical toxins and hormones that helps to make us feel better. Ever notice that after a good cry, you feel better? The reason for the tears still exists, but the release of the harmful toxins in exchange for the good endorphins allows this good feeling to happen. I often cried when I lost my loved ones. It seemed like crying was the only thing that I could do well for a while. Each time was just one more opportunity to express the boundless love that I have for my loved ones. I used to feel guilty for crying so much. I wanted to be strong because I knew my family wanted me to be strong. So if you need to cry, go ahead and shed those tears. Let nothing hold you back. The benefit I found from letting the tears flow is that crying has a soothing effect on us as it activates our parasympathetic nervous system. Crying dulls the pain of loss; it helps you recover from the loss, and it's also a rallying cry for support. Just remember, you're not alone. The Bible tells us in Revelation 21:4 that God will wipe all tears from our eyes and there will be no more death. That's the beautiful promise that I carry with me each day. It's your promise as well if you choose to accept it.

Talk, Talk, Talk. Like tears, talking can be one of the best ways to heal. If you find you are concerned that people may not want to be around you much if you're always talking about your loved one, find a special friend willing to help you through the grieving process. Staying silent is not an option you should consider. In the long run, it offers you nothing. When needed, don't shy away from seeking a professional. On the occasions I talked about my loved ones with others, it helped ease some of the emotional weight I sometimes carried around unwittingly. The more I spoke, the more I recognized the areas that caused me great pain. Today when I talk about my losses, people are amazed by how I see things now. Sometimes I chuckle to myself because I know that it is only by the grace of God and a dedicated prayer life that I can talk the way that I talk now. I live and meditate on the promises of Revelation 21:4 and 1Thesselonians 4:16-18. These promises I offer to you.

What do you need to get off your chest?

_____

_____

_____

_____

_____

_____

_____

_____

_____

_____

_____

_____

_____

_____

_____

These are the No's No's

Don't make any significant decisions. Unless not making a decision would lead to a catastrophe, it is best not to make any critical decisions while at the onset of grief. Often we may feel like we need to change everything to cope. I get it. I wanted to move to someplace different because I thought it would be easier for me. However, I came to realize that moving was not the answer. I was grieving, and moving to a different place would not change that because wherever I go, I would always be. If it's not critical, you don't have to decide anything. Give yourself time to consider everything before you make significant decisions. If you find that you must make a critical decision, seek the advice of a close friend or relative. I made some hasty decisions of which I later regretted making. Ask yourself, if you didn't decide, what would you lose. If the answer is you would not lose anything that would further upset your well-being, then hold off for your good. There will be plenty of time for decision-making in the months to come.

No Chemicals Allowed. It may be tempting to turn to outside stimulants such as alcohol, illegal or prescribed drugs to lessen the pain, but these can lead you down a path you had not intended. The greater the pain we experience, the greater the stimulants we need to numb the pain. It's best to avoid these altogether. I realize that this may prove difficult for some, and should you find yourself in this situation, please seek professional help. Outside stimulants have never been able to erase emotional pain. Practicing some of the other exercises mentioned can positively affect you.

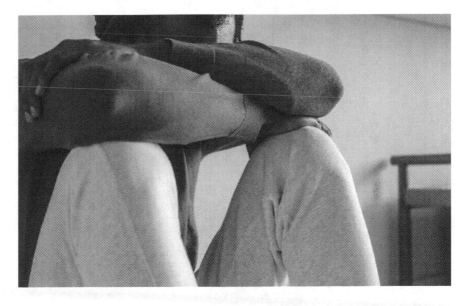

No feelings of guilt. This one is the real zinger. Nothing can tear you down more than feelings of guilt or responsibility. I remember these feelings after my middle sister and my husband died. I couldn't help but think that there was something more I should have done. Intellectually I knew that the cause of their death was way beyond my control, but that didn't stop me from having those guilty feelings nonetheless. Remember, there will be plenty of 'I should have' or 'I wish I would have.' I must have run that scenario in my head hundreds of times after my last sister died unexpectedly. I've learned that you can't beat yourself up about the things that did not happen, no matter the reason. There is no value there. Instead, filter through the halls of your mind and find all of the good things that did happen. Let those memories become food for your thought, building blocks for your body, and healing for your spirit. You must leave no room in your life for feelings of guilt or responsibility.

What if anything are you feeling guilty about?

_____

_____

_____

_____

_____

_____

_____

_____

_____

_____

_____

_____

_____

Don't Go Into Hiding. I know what you think about this because I've been there more times than I wish I had. The last thing you want is to extend yourself or be around others. Your instinct is to withdraw or retreat. We do this because we believe that others don't know how we feel. Well, it's true others don't know how you feel, but I'm pretty sure a friend is willing to be there for you. Get with your friends or make a new friend. Do whatever it takes to get back into society by any healthy means necessary. But be sure to allow yourself time to grieve.

The Light Will Shine Again

Losing the ones we love is perhaps the most challenging thing we will ever have to endure in this life. I believe it is so because there are no rulebooks or guidelines that we can follow to make things better. Sure we can gain encouragement from others that have been down the same road, but each individual's experience is different. I had to connect to a higher power source to endure and move forward. When I joined with that source, I found that I could transcend the earthly. Like mine, the light will shine again in your life. Let your every effort be to move in the direction of the light.

Moving towards the light can be challenging. To get close to the light, I had to plan for those special days that only came once a year. Instead of feelings of sorrow when special days were approaching, I decided to meet them head-on with plans to celebrate them. Here are some things that can help you move in the direction of the light. Try them and see how they work for you.

1. Honor your loved one's memory. Celebrating special days is an excellent time to be creative. You can find an assortment of your loved ones' favorite things, make a scrapbook, collage, or even put it in a display case. Become a volunteer at their favorite charity or donate funds to help support it. Whatever you do, let it be the gift that keeps on giving. The possibilities are endless.

2. Plan for special occasions. If you're anything like me, you hate to be caught unprepared. I am very much a planner. You know those special occasions are coming so why not plan for them. If you plan for birthdays, holidays, and anniversaries, you're more likely to have more success in getting through them without feelings of dread. Planning does not mean you won't have feelings of sadness. It merely helps you take the stress out of stressfull and leave you full of good memories. Be sure to involve family and friends if needed.

3. Visit places you went together. When you're ready, this one can be very uplifting. There is a sense of being close to your loved one in its unique way. Your mind can recall the time you spent there together. I always feel happy when I visit the beach because that is one of the places I enjoyed immensely with my husband. We had lots of dates on the beach.

4. Hang out with Family and Friends. Grieving is already a hard enough process to navigate. Don't make the process harder by isolating yourself from others. Spend as much time as you can in the company of family and friends. Trust me; there will be plenty of midnights when you will find yourself all alone. Fill up on the good times to have the fuel to sustain you in those midnight hours.

5. Express Yourself. Good things often come out of not-so-good things. Though I would never choose to have something good happen in my life at the expense of something terrible happening to

a loved one, life finds a way sometimes to present us with the very things we don't want. I used to write when I was much younger. The loss of some exceptional people in my life has brought back the writer in me. As I write, I can feel the healing process in my spirit. If my words can cause this same reaction for others as they read them, I would count them as a good thing. Why not try taking some time out to discover how you can express yourself.

Learn to Enjoy Life Again

Finally, I say to those who have lost loved ones, don't despair or lose hope. Life is so much more than what is summed up in death because death is only the end of this life. At the right time, you will start to enjoy life again and not feel guilty about it. Love is worthy of us grieving when we lose our loved ones. But, it is also worthy of us living. God has seen fit for us to be here still, so let's not waste the time we have to make a difference. We have many choices before us to make. Let us choose life.

Additional Activities

- Learn to forgive others and yourself***
- Treasure the fond memories***
- Go swimming
- Join an activities club
- Get plenty of rest
- Drinks lots of water***
- Complete unfinished business
- Join a book club
- Clean the house (yep, I said it)***
- Play with the kid outside (be sure to stretch first)
- Listen to your favorite music***
- After listening, sing your favorite songs as loud as you can***
- After singing, dance the night away
- Take a long drive up the coast***
- Take up cooking or baking lessons
- Exercise***
- Teach your favorite subject
- Take up boxing
- Do indulge in lots of comedy (ok you can add some chocolate)***
- Look at old photographs***
- Start counting your blessing***
- Keep an attitude of gratitude***
- Start journaling or writing***

- Find a hiding place to be alone with your thoughts – but don't get lost there
- Enjoy a day of no rules and no schedules to keep***
- Do things that make you laugh (it really is the best medicine)***
- Photography

***These were the things that brought the most joy to me

Writing Exercises

As you write down your responses, ask yourself if your response is true. If it is true, can you still hold on to them, accomplish them or let them go.

1) What made your loved one(s) special to you?

A)

B)

C)

2) What things did your loved one(s) do that always made you laugh?

A)

B)

C)

3) What things did your loved one(s) want to see you accomplish?

A)

B)

C)

4) In what ways did your loved one(s) make you a better person?

A)

B)

C)

5) What are you most thankful for?

A)

B)

C)

About the Author

Valencia McMahon

I was always the shyest of my mother's three daughters, yet somehow, I've overcome most of that shyness during the last 11 years. God has been better than good to me because he blessed me with Cash McMahon, a very special person who shared 10 ½ of those last 11 years with me. He grew to become my best friend, my confidant and my husband. It was his love, his constant encouragement and his winning spirit that caused me to try things I had not done before. He was that light in my life that God lovingly placed there. Although I have lost four of the most important people in my life, which are both sisters, my mother and then my husband, I still have God on my side and in my heart. It is He who sustains me daily. And though my words can never convey the loss that I feel, nor the hope that burns within my heart, God has given me the words within this book to share with others to help ease their pain.